WAITING FOR DEATH TO COME

AND OTHER DARK POEMS

LEIGH HADDINGTON

TOMBTOME PUBLISHERS

Copyright © 2021 Leigh Haddington for Tombtome Publishing

Cover Artwork by GrandFailure.

Sign Language Artwork by Hein Nouwens

All rights reserved

No part of this book may be reproduced in any form or by any electronic or mechanical means, including information storage and retrieval systems, without written permission from the author, except for the use of brief quotations in a book review.

Dedicated to the demons in my head, you know who you are.

And to room 217.

FOREWORD

When I began to work on my poetry craft, it was to develop my writing. I wanted to try and add a lyrical flow to my creative writing. I feel like it has helped. During writing the second novel, I noticed areas where I would play with sentences differently than I would have in my debut novel. My mind started to work in a way that pushed me to express an image clearer than before.

As I have always believed, poetry is like a polaroid photo, a snapshot of a moment, then within time fades. You need to capture that moment, keep it clear, tell a story in a small picture frame. I feel like I have achieved that in the majority of poems in this book. Hopefully, this time, containing a little more colour and maybe, a little more life too.

The inspiration for these poems come from word prompts on Twitter, a story I have read somewhere, memories bubbling to the surface once in a while, or just my imagination. Some topics I touch on, the more macabre side, obviously is not from experience. Let me get that clear before anyone starts wanting

FOREWORD

to dig up my garden looking for remains. No, they are all at my allotment if you would like to dig that up.

My poetry books are created solely by myself. I acquire the artwork from Adobe Stock Art, as I did with this cover. This artwork is by an artist only known as GrandFailure, a fantastic artist. I saw it, and it inspired another poem. I do this myself, so I can see my work develop, grow, improve. I need to show that anyone can do this, spread your wings, fly!

I hope you find something in these polaroids, even if it's just a distraction for an hour or two from the fucked up, crazy life we are all living at the moment.

WAITING FOR DEATH TO COME

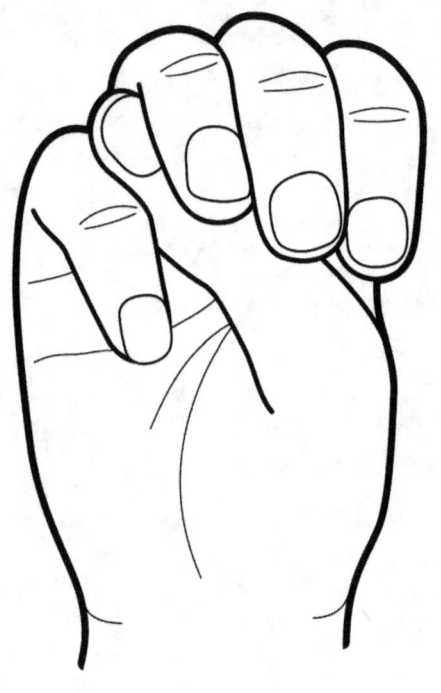

A SHADOW

He explained that they had found a shadow,
something that shouldn't be there.
Something they want to look closer at,
it's something that needs extra care.
The Doctor said he doesn't think it's anything to worry about
after all the pain hasn't been there for long.
And once they had had a closer look,
he's sure it's nothing he's not usually wrong.
So, they opened me up and poked inside
the surgeons gathered round.
Incoherent whisperings,
faces of sadness abound.
The Doctor explained to me afterwards
he was very sorry there was nothing they could do.
My loneliness, depression, self-hatred had got too much,
and that is something I already knew.

AGE

There is a preconceived notion
that a man at my age
shouldn't pen emotion.
That he shouldn't share his thoughts,
his rage in a safe place.
Letting the blood from my quill spill
my words speaking of sour ill,
my jealousy, hatred or love.
Should I give up?
Haven't I done enough?
My darkest thoughts,
nobody needs to see the gore.
After all, what's it all been for?

ALEXA DROP IN

"Alexa drop in"
"Drop into Leigh's 2nd Echo?"
"Yes"
"Hi Mum, it's Leigh..."
"..."
"I just thought I would let you know, I miss you. I really fucking miss you."
"..."
"Say hi to Dad."
"..."
"Bye Mum"
"...I'm sorry I can't connect you to Leigh's 2nd Echo."
"... I know. Alexa, can I use you as an ouija board or a medium?"

ANOMALY

There is something wrong with me,
I have said it all along.
I feel like my soul is slipping
and my grasp isn't that strong
I can feel the darkness taking hold,
feel the crazies devour me.
I just hope I can control it,
my twisted, strangling, anomaly.

AVOIDANCE

I see you every day,
eye contact brings avoidance.
When did we lose each other?
A lack of benevolence.
Have we ever been close?
Always disappointing.
Your achievements mean nothing!
How can you love anything?
I shouldn't have mirrors,
my head doesn't need help.
With the constant voices,
my mind can make enemies itself.

BEE

My skin crawls
with a parasitic symphony,
shapes beneath
eating at flesh and tissue.
And I lie here paralysed,
wishing the horror would stop.
Praying for the light,
praying for my curtain to drop.
Then the morning comes
and I am glad to be alive,
knowing tonight the swarm will return
only to become their living human beehive.

BEHIND THE ABUSED

Some call me a liar,
a twister of the truth.
A causer of misery,
I stand behind the abused.
Did I hurt you?
If so, I don't care.
I speak so much bull
they call me a centaur.
And Just so you know,
I sleep through the night.
I'm antisocial,
and I always bring the fight.
I will always tell you
what you need to hear.
I will hide
in your darkest fears.
I'll wait till you're alone
and the darkness clings.
Then I will wrap you up,
in my blackened wings.

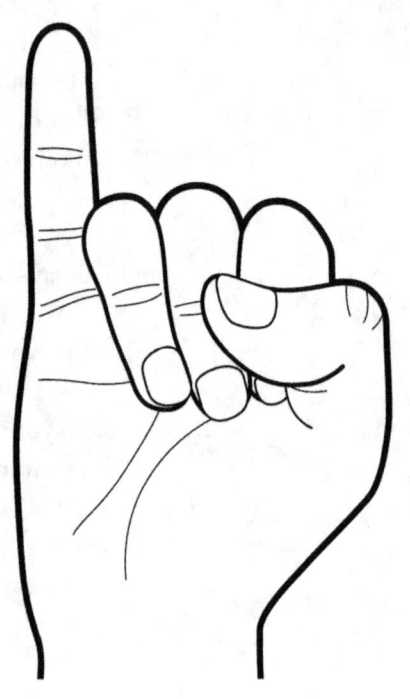

BELONG

There's a moment in the madness,
when I finally breakthrough.
Where the clouds start to clear,
and I see you for you.
I see through the scars,
through the hexes, the voodoo,
to the charred remains of your heart,
and the poisoned words you brew.
Forgive me if I sound heartless,
and I have got everything wrong.
But that's the reflection I get,
in the mirror, knowing I don't belong.

BINDINGS

Kidnapped,
chained to your radiator,
shackled to your narcotic heat.
Your bindings cut,
and I yearn for my release.
You tell me that you don't hold me,
that I am not your captive.
Yet, there is one thing that remains true,
if I could escape,
I would only run to you.

BLIND FAITH

Blind faith is a moment
where your stupidity takes over
Belief is a moment
Where your soul is in control

BLOCK

Stagnation crawls through my mind
like a hammer house mist.
Enveloping every creative idea,
swallowing each twist.
Every image of direction,
each plot conceived.
Has been eaten by the fog
no longer to be seen.
Then, there's a spark,
a glimmer of hope.
Movement, a swirl, a whisp,
a face seeps through
and a word spoken
a narration,
a story,
a kiss.

BLUE TACK

Fleeting moments,
happiness, misery.
Blue Tacked to our walls,
covering the cracks.
On display to lift you,
Or destroy you.
Occasionally they drop,
leaving you in shock,
knowing the Blue Tack won't hold.
Knowing it isn't a sufficient amount to keep your memories
together.
Your naked wall, bearing the cracks for all to see,
deep, damaging, blooded cracks.
Your memories,
trying not to forget.
But the blue tack won't hold,
and you eventually give up,
leaving them scattered on your floors,
trampled, torn, ripped,
left to be thrown in the bin.

BROKEN SWITCH

There's a switch in my head,
I think it's broken.
It controls the drainage plug,
it control's my buoyancy.
I think it's defective.
Like anybody, it stays on,
but mine will switch off,
for no reason.
And down I go,
drowning in the depths,
taking in water,
struggling to exist.
Then it switches back on, and I'm ok.
I can breathe again,
for no fucking reason.
I think it needs fixing,
but I don't know how to.

BURTON AGNES HALL

I was never one to believe,
that our lives intertwine through time.
But as I ascended the staircase,
such beauty caught my eye.
Your portrait hung high
and dominated a vastness of the wall.
The familiarity of your eyes
embraced my living soul.
I felt such sorrow
and yearning in my heart.
For we were once lovers,
in a past life until your death tore us apart.
But now my existence,
is a lifetime from your call,
or is that why your skull once screamed
in Burton Agnes Hall.

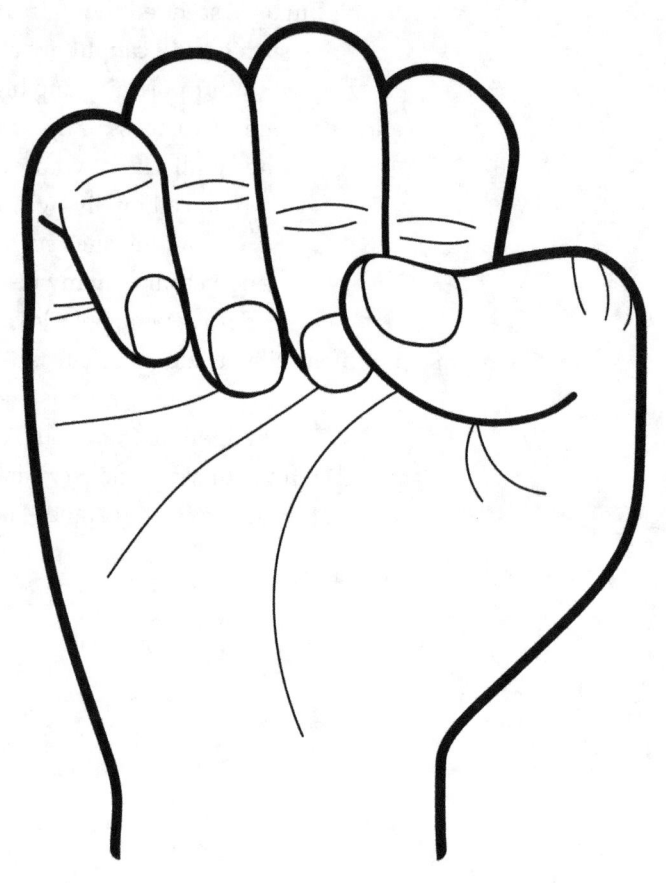

CANINES

My bite, my bark,
Canines, tearing for your heart.
Slashing, ripping,
destruction of your chest.
Smashing through your rib cage,
blooded by the mess.
It beats, I plunge,
your life I crush.
Always driven by blood lust.

CHOICES

Bad choices define us
We aren't made from the good choices
It's the scars
The pain the hurt
"I really shouldn't"
"maybe this is too far"
You shouldn't and yes it is too far
Yet it feels so good
Any choice you will regret
But the bad ones stick around
Was it worth it?
Probably not but at the time
Well, you know how good that felt.
Regret always follows though
Always there eating at you
Licking its lips
Tasting
Was it worth it?
Not really, not now.

CONTRACT

With each word written
my ancient blood spilt.
From generation to generation
my ancestry stains the parchment,
scrawled from the quill.
This moment I embrace,
a coiled serpent
wrapped around my history,
squeezing, spilling my blood.
My hunger, my willingness,
my life, my whole.
The deal complete
you have my soul.
I sit and wait for my reward,
my two pieces of shiny gold.

CORNER

I can see you,
you, hiding in the corner,
deep in your tenebrous,
watching me.
I can hear you,
you, screaming my name,
silently waiting,
listening to me.
I do know you,
your darkest fear,
covering your face,
studying me.
I am you,
you, cowering from myself,
swallowed in my shadows,
lost to me.

CUTTING

Scratching at the surface,
movement under my skin.
The itching is unbearable,
the world beneath is sin.
The shaking of my soul,
my inner hope won't sing.
I can feel my organs crumble,
I won't let the voices win.
I put the blade to my flesh,
I let the cutting begin.
No blood for me to shed,
just the darkness from within.

DEEP FRIED

There are times when I see your smile,
and recall your mesmerising stare.
The touch of your fingers tips,
as they caress through my hair.
I carry these memories,
buried deep inside.
Just like your heart, your kidney and your liver,
all devoured, all deep fried.

DESIRE OF LONELINESS

Time crawls and my heart yearns,
not for you, but the loss of you.
Every moment together
I'm blinded by the inevitable heartache.
I crave the blackness, the sorrow,
the way my chest aches,
my speech breaks
and the loneliness of tomorrow.
The shedding of my burnt soul,
restoration of my internal hole.
It's time to let go,
time to start again.
It was never the love that I needed,
just a reason to bleed.

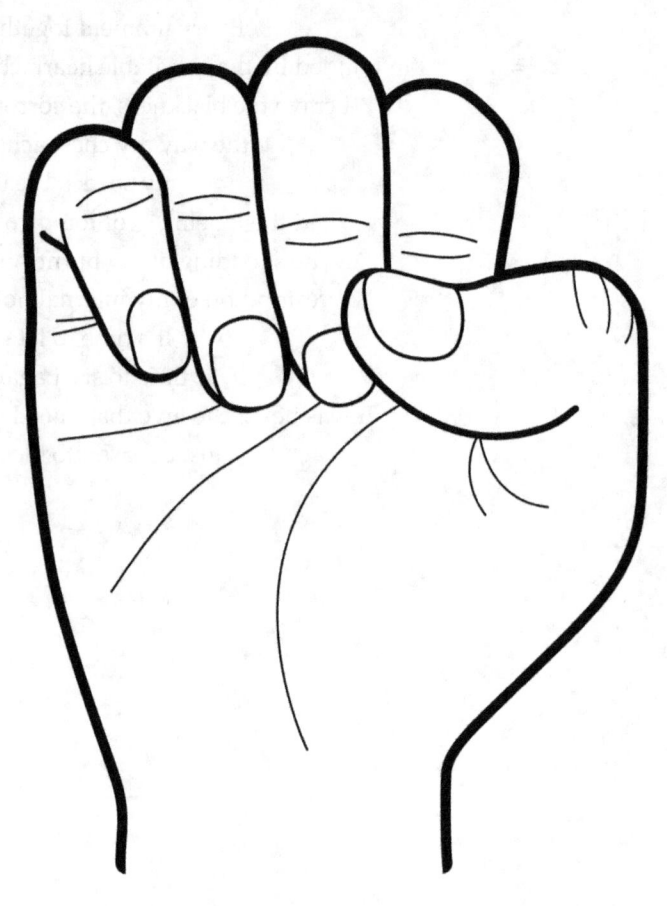

DISEASED

I have had enough of this fucking world,
I have been scratched by its constant disease.
The hatred we as humans spread,
contagious, unforgivable beliefs.
Destroying our planet in the name of progress,
tearing the beauty from its veins.
Nuclear power disasters,
global warming, acid rain.
If only we could live in peace, together,
the way nature intended.
The chance to live as one,
until the planet is mended.

DUG

I dug up my past yesterday
I should have left it longer
The image of the rotting flesh was bad
But the rotting smell was stronger

ENGLAND

The pigs are loose,
uncaged, unchained,
mayhem and filth,
their mob mentality;
the hatred supreme.
Stop them, block them;
corporate entities are living the dream.
Delusion of your entitlement,
the primitive emojis are not intelligent.
Childish tantrums,
"I didn't get what I want."
hate-filled fist stomps.
They are not fit to be human
their opinion doesn't show you who I am.
Because I am proud of you,
proud of your journey,
your charity and loyalty,
your power, your empathy.
For carrying us in your hand
and showing us the love we have in England.

ERUPTION

Slashed wrists,
spilt blood,
broken heart,
emotional flood.
Pain eruption,
suffocating hood,
poisoned soul,
rejected love.
Notice my sacrifice,
notice my cuts,
watch me tear myself to pieces,
watch me die for you.

FIGHTING DEPRESSION

Fighting depression
is a solo blood sport.
Hiding from yourself,
avoiding being caught.
Bare knuckles
and raw nerves.
Being made of scars
is only what I deserve.
Moments of clarity,
moments of victory.
Then a shank to the rib cage
and your clarity is history.
Internally crippled,
victory stripped.
Another loss chalked up,
my soul left ripped.

FORGET

Fragmented memories,
your last few days prominent.
I forget sometimes,
and I need to tell you something,
then I recall,
and the floor leaves.
For a split second, you're still there.
I forget your voice,
Dads too, I know I shouldn't,
I try to remember but, I forget.
I forget everything, not always,
not the last few days,
your gripping hands.
Did you know we were there?
I am always there.

FORTRESS

I walk your dreams, unseen.
Your unwanted wishes,
your desolate desires.
The emotionless fortress,
the untouched passions,
your forgotten lusts.
I walk your dreams, unseen.

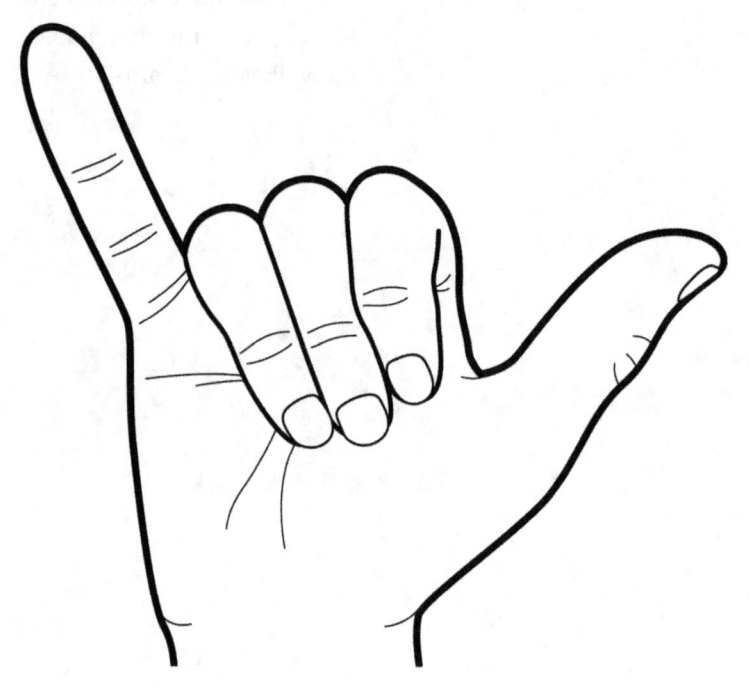

FROST

I heard it in the whisper,
in your moans,
your final choking
blood gurgling moment.
I heard the words.
Like mist rising on a cold winter morning
As the low sun hits the frost.
The words I needed to hear,
bloodstained and curdled with fear.
As your colour drained,
and your desperation to live peaked.
Your last breath whispered,
"I hate you!"

FUTURE

Would life be better
If you knew your end?
If you knew your fate
What's around the bend?
A countdown clock
Timing your demise
Knowing the day, the time
With no surprise?
Could you enjoy your life?
Be comfortable with your path?
With time to plan,
A chance to write your epitaph?
Or would you try to change your doom?
To redirect the outcome?
To stop the hands of time?
To change the game you haven't won?
But we don't know,
And thank God life is a mystery
Because we will all die one day
And we all become history.

GENTLY

Gently, she lay her down,
motionless and drained.
A picture of disfigurement
in a moment of beauty.
She knew this might not work,
but she waited,
seconds decomposed.
She waited but sanguine.
Then a spasm,
a crack in this frozen moment.
Her chest thrust forward,
and the birth of a new terror unleashed.
An eternal love.
Her corruption of God was forever.
Let the blood flow.

GODLESS

I pull my fingers from your eyes,
you're grasping for my soul.
I watch your body writhing,
my excitement explodes.
Nothing natural intended,
gruesome with every cut.
I see your blood, your guts,
your pain with every blow struck.
I leave you as a Limp quivering mess,
pounded, bleeding, a slab of nothingness.
You're a disfigured entity, unrecognisable,
I am pure evil, I am godless.

GRIP

I have worshipped your presence,
the air that carried your essence.
The fragrance from your aura,
enchanted by your movements,
your strength, your weakness.
The smoothness of your neck,
The power of my hands,
my grip.
I need your breath,
your heart pounding slower in your chest,
your limpness.
Then I release,
and you breathe again.

HAUNTED MEDICATION

Alone, I sit in this shell of a house,
drugs to keep me awake,
more drugs to stop the shake.
And I grip my gun,
I wait for the night to come.
For the demons to arrive,
screeching for my life.
I don't know how long I have sat here,
might be a minute, an hour,
a day or a week.
I can't seem to remember,
but they will come; they always do.
Now and then, someone will pass by and ask if I'm ok?
I tell them the same thing every day,
"only when they stop!" But they never stop.
More drugs, no shake.

Am I awake?

HIDING

My soul always hides in the darkness,
and the darkness hides in my soul.
No matter how loud I scream
the darkness always keeps alone.
Tortured and mutilated,
my mind lies and betrays my heart,
it whispers,
"don't worry, everything will be fine."

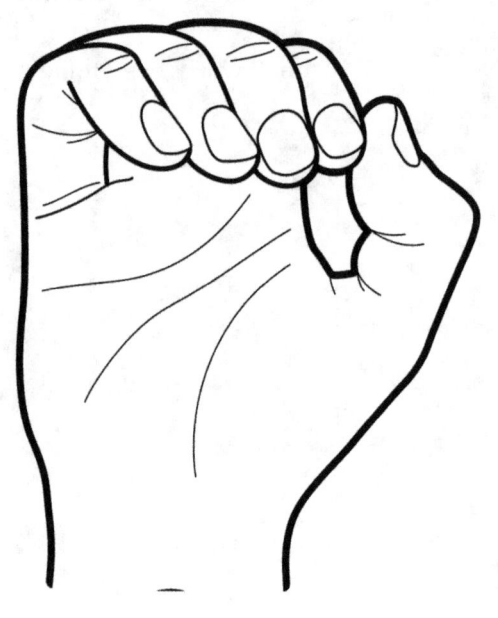

HOOKS

Fish hooks under my skin,
pulling,
dragging me in.
I cut,
slice,
peel back,
expose my cracks.
My flaws,
no life hacks.
Dramatised suicide,
for the YouTube views,
for new shoes.
Soulless, clueless,
on the edge, waiting for the push.
Aching to be seen,
living the dream,
even with razor blades in your bloodstreams.

HOPE

Why should I hold out for hope?
In a world
that wants you to choke,
that wants you to die by your sword.
Every day, losing yards
forced through no man's land.
Anxiety, courage is torn apart,
trying to stand and not die by your words.
If I was to overcome,
stand tall, be proud,
take the world and lift the shroud.
You would still hold tight,
crush my windpipe,
and stop my desire to explode.
Why should I hold out for hope?

HORROR OF THE GRAVEYARD WATCHER

As I tiptoed through the cemetery,
tapping on each tombstone.
Waking up the residents,
filling the night with moans.
I stumbled upon a little girl,
somehow lost in the moonlight.
I whispered, "Evening, little girl, Are you lost? What brings
you out here tonight?"
No words she spoke
and fumbled with her dress.
Her innocent eyes looked up
that's when I noticed the distress.
I asked her, "What's the matter, little girl?
Can't you find your mummy?"
Then with a deep voice, that of a beast,
she said, "I'm going to put you in my tummy!"
I ran like an antelope,
leaping from tomb to tomb,
avoiding all the apparitions,
trying not to be consumed.
And then it happened,
I tripped, and my shoe fell off.
She was on me in a second,
and that was that.
I was scoffed!

HUMIEN

Brush strokes gracefully explores
the curves, curls, bewitching human.
Strong, balanced, gentle,
Creating heaven, artistic alien.

IMPLODE

I wonder how many scars your heart can hold
before it implodes?
How many cuts and rips your soul can bear
before it corrodes?
How long can you sit in silence
and accept your decline?
Taking all the kicks and punches,
hoping that all's fine?
Do you have to listen to the constant attacks,
knowing the dagger is blunt?
Or is it time to rise and take control
and strangle the fucking cunt?

IMPOSTER

Look at you,
believing your lies.
Keep telling yourself
your greatness is yet to come.
You belittle me; ignore me,
I try and tell you that you are no good.
Tell you that you're nothing,
yet you call me captious,
but I am just trying to help.
You say imposter,
I say improver.
Ignore me,
hate me.
I will always be here,
to remind you,
you will always be nothing.

LIAR

I see you broken, bleeding,
and I wrap my shadows around you.
The warmth of my darkness,
the need in your tears.
I pull you in closer,
your acceptance of my words.
I wipe the pain from your cheeks,
and I caress your hair and I tell you.
"Everything will be ok,
Everything will be fine."
I lie.
Every second you stay in my darkness,
every second I drain your power.
Every second you love me,
every second you die.
I lie.
You die.

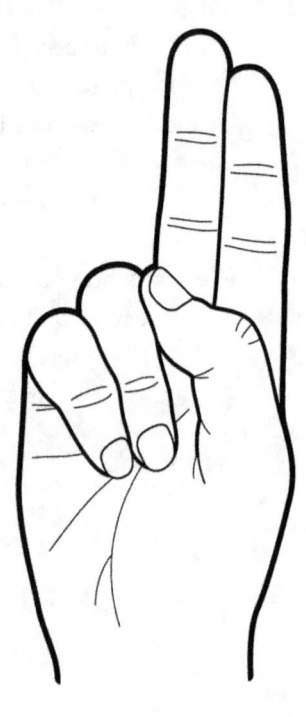

LIZARD KING

The innocence of youth,
craving for a life of indulgence.
To be a God of words,
unsurpassed confidence.
Touch of a demon,
the passion of a whore.
Wisdom of a Sharman,
leaving them aching for more.
Never grow old,
desired always.
To be a memory of seduction,
carried to the grave.

MASQUERADE

I live a life in seclusion,
away from prying eyes.
Hiding from the day,
waiting for the moonlight.
My life is a masquerade ball,
a macabre dance of hell.
Violence and bloodshed,
too horrific for me to tell.
I watch from the shadows
waiting for my next prey.
My existence is to predate
and to sleep my days away.

MISSING

Today I see I am invisible,
lost in the corner of your vision.
Unrecognisable, unremarkable,
forgettable, missing.
I have known this for some time,
watched my essence fade.
Translucent in the crowd,
I am no one, I will disappear in the haze.

MONSTER

As a child, I would run up our stairs,
up the stairs to bed from the living room.
It wasn't for my health or the love of exercise,
but the creature who would bring me my doom.
The creature wasn't caused by a childhood trauma
or a member of my family.
But the shadows in the hallway
that would stretch out and peel the skin from me.
This went on through my childhood,
it would never leave me alone.
Until the day I outgrew it
and I could finally leave home.
Now I'm in my forties
and I now own my parent's homestead.
I find myself each night as I cross the hall,
I still look over my shoulder on my way to bed.

MUSCLE OF LOVE

The love you once had,
and the love you gave.
Your heart offered to others,
promised till the grave.
Oh, how the feeling surged through your body,
beating with every kiss.
You told yourself that this was your Everest,
your stomach butterflies, your teenage bliss.
But, now, as I hold it,
dripping with blood and veins.
I question your use of it,
as your life quickly drains.
Did you wear it on your sleeve,
a beacon of your state of mind?
Did you promise it to everyone,
just in case you got left behind?
Did you give it away cheaply,
as you offered it to me?
Just a stranger in the night,
here to set you free.
But only now do you realise,
that this muscle only pounds
to maintain your body to give it life,
now useless, leaving you dead on the ground.

MY DARK WITCH

I knew it would be my death,
but the taste of her lips was so sweet.
Soft, cherry and corrosive,
my world set alight, I fell at her feet.
The touch of her youthful virus,
poison burned my eyes.
She embraced my wretched soul,
my dark witch, my suicide.

NIGHT TERRORS

Cradled in your unholy soul,
I lay motionless, speechless, trapped.
Your hands explore, nails dig, scratch, tear.
Heart racing and your tendrils pull me in,
I am paralysed, crippled by your symbiosis.
Your parasitic lust, need to terrorise my sleep.

NO RAIN

Some moments happen in your life,
that make you take a pause.
That stays with you forever,
that playback in your thoughts.
These moments appear to you,
that you just don't expect.
Those moments where there's no one else,
and repeat for you to reflect.
A moment shared between just the two of you,
a moment on your mind, stained.
A moment of perfect memory,
a moment of no rain.

PARIS

Did you see me dead,
asleep in my casket?
Was I a beautiful corpse?
Grotesque and empty?
Was I the wine you drank at my wake,
a celebration in my honour?
Or was the memory too hard,
too fractious to swallow?

PARTS

There are parts of me,
broken and torn, dragged from me.
Bits of me that I didn't want anymore,
the scar tissue of bad choices.
Parts that when I think about them,
I feel my spine being pulled out vertebrae by vertebrae,
the times when I fucked up.
I could see the pain stained on those pictures,
carved in my soul.
Reminding me in the darkness,
in the silence of slumber.
Things that I had forgotten,
that I wanted to forget.
Yeah, I tore those pieces out,
my bare, bleeding fingertips,
pulling the raised, hate-filled scars,
leaving a chasm in its place.
Time goes by, and I wonder why I have a blackened void,
And I remember,
I see the raised, hate-filled scars again,
left to remind me that I fucked up
and to never forget it.

PAST EATS

Am I ok today?
I mean,
has yesterday's pain gone away?
Passed on like mist?
Evaporated, faded?
Or do I still feel self-hatred?
Crazy as it sounds,
I still hear those voices,
the loathing, goading
of my memories, my present,
my past, they all harassed.
Replaying the shit,
my broken bits,
ashamed of my mistakes.
They never let go,
they never stop replaying the show,
never.
But, in my defence
there has never been intent
to make it go away.
So you ask, am I ok?
Has the pain gone today?
No, it never will,
but I'm ok with that bitter pill.

POETRY

I have realised no one likes my poetry,
I can't even sell a single book.
I mean, I'm not doing it for the money,
my bank manager couldn't give a fuck.
I do it for something deeper,
something more primal than that.
I do it for my ego, for the reviews,
you know for the pat on the back.
I can't help being this way,
it was the way that god had planned it.
For me to be jealous of everyone else,
for their mass of sales and the plaudits.
My self-belief always told me no,
the imposter was right.
And if I honestly look deep inside,
I would see that my poetry is shite.
But I keep going,
still putting out the rhymes.
Peeling away a section of my soul
each time I commit my crimes.

POLAROIDS

Half written poems,
half exposed polaroids.
Half of a vivid dream,
of a conversation with no voice.
The sight of the blind,
the music of the deaf.
The rage of my scream
caught under my breath.

POWDER

I lift it to my mouth,
feel the shape touch my lips
and it grazes my teeth on its way in.
The taste makes me feel like shit,
determination pushes me through.
I am not sure where things changed,
where the desire came from,
when my thoughts became deranged.
But I'm here on my knees,
the voice has said its last word,
with this barrel in my mouth.
I shake and my finger twitches,
panic and fear hit me,
and my finger twitches again.
A loud noise chokes my hearing.
The taste of metal powder,
and the sledgehammer hits my throat.
Faster than a speeding bullet
that lasts a lifetime.
My screen goes blank
and finally, all the dots join.

Please insert coin.

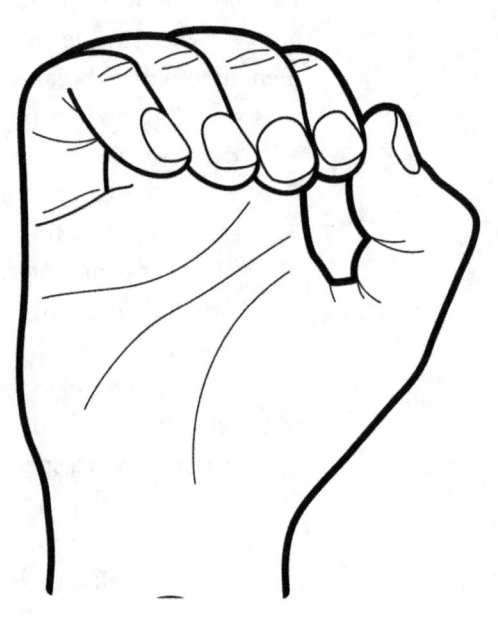

PRIDE

It doesn't take a month
to show your worth,
your individuality.
I already know your power,
even if you don't.
You begin your journey,
a traveller alone,
in a crowd, marching to a dream.
Let's embrace your future,
strive through the pain.
You are a wonderful human,
a beautiful soul.
I envy your strength,
your fight to be true.
This may be your first month of pride,
but I have always been proud of you.

PUMPKIN

Here I am again left on your stoop,
hiding behind my positive smile.
Like a pumpkin at Halloween,
gutted and disposed of,
left to rot in the autumn sun.
I am fine in the knowledge that this is temporary,
I know you will be back to carve my soul
and light my flame once more.

RISE ABOVE

The greatest gift
We can give our kids
Are a pair of wings
The freedom to rise
To soar, to fall
To learn from every sting
No greater gift
For any parent
Is to watch their child fly
To embrace the storm
To rise above, never fall
To be rulers of their sky

SEVENTEEN

Stability is critical on the rail,
close the door, use the wedge.
Grapple with the belt,
the balance on the bath edge.
My feelings explained,
my reasons why.
All the Chitta, Chatta, in my head,
the voices must die.
I keep my words to myself,
but I know you can hear.
Like a transmitter radio,
my thoughts are broadcasted clear.
I scrawl my images for you,
my world etched.
My diary explains my decay,
my bloodshed.
I take my final step,
my final portrait complete.
My veins opened for all the world,
my ending anything but sweet.

SHOELESS FEET

I promised today would be my last.
I have delved into my dark flowing soul,
burnt my last bridge
and now I am here.
Shoeless feet,
sand on my toes.
Lungs ready,
I wait for the waves,
the warmth of the freezing depths,
If you saw me, would you reach out?
A gesture, help?
Or would you watch?
Watch my world die.
You only watch.
Watch me stretch to you?
Watch me yearn?
I hope you learn from my closure,
as they drag me to shore.
I wonder, would you stand here with me?
Shoeless feet,
sand on your toes.

SILENT

Drifting through the darkness,
in the solitude of your mind.
Leaving stained memories
of recollections left behind.
The moments of sickness,
bleeding from the cracks.
Seeping from the shadows,
trapped in horrifying flashbacks.
Twitching, shaking,
dragging for the kill,
static on the radio,
never to return from Silent Hill.

SLEEP

His teeth embed,
in this soul of dread.
His fingers dig deep,
bringing his incubus sleep.
Cocooned in his hearse,
his poisonous curse.
There is no escape,
of his nocturnal grave.

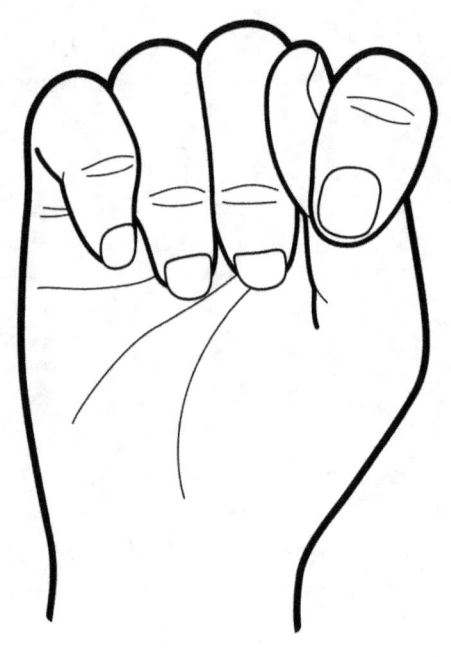

SMILE

They say a smile can be infectious.
Well, I've had a enough of infections,
And smiles.

SOMETIMES

Sometimes I imagine
lying in bed,
staring at the four walls
trying to be dead.
Sometimes I imagine
the world is on fire,
my skin flailing from my flesh
the angels take me higher.
Sometimes I imagine
all hell has been let loose,
the demons rule the world
and I'm hanging from a noose,
Sometimes I imagine
I have a regular 9-5,
the boredom destroying my soul
wishing I wasn't alive.

STITCHES

A stitch comes loose,
and I spill my stuffing.
Cover it up
you don't need to see it.
I'm defective,
You can't see that.
I need to keep it hidden,
I don't want to be trash.
Threadbare,
carelessly you cared.
Close to spill,
I hide my transparencies.
I know I'm disposable,
easily replaceable,
barely loveable.
Pick me up,
pass the needle through.
Repair my faults,
make me new.

TO FLY

There are days I get down,
feel the grinding pain.
I know I'm not easy to be around,
and I'm a permanent drain.
Some days it's harder,
and I'm just not that strong.
To drag me through the shit,
with the feeling, I don't belong.
Then come the days where I know,
that I'm doing alright.
And I'm getting through this,
that I might be winning the fight.
I stand up and lift my head,
and I shout to the sky.
"Today I want to live,
Today I want to FLY!"

WAIT

They say in life, two things are guaranteed,
taxes and death.
Well, I disagree with one thing anyway,
the taxes part.
I think waiting and death are two things that are guaranteed.
Sit and wait,
waiting for something to happen,
anything,
just waiting for the event.
For the arrival,
for the loss,
for the happiness.
Waiting, just fucking waiting.
I wait for your reply.
Yep, waiting and death, welcome to reality.

WAITING FOR DEATH TO COME

I watch the dark crimson rain,
brain and pain,
washed away.
My life ejected,
never resurrected.
It's the best thing really,
you will see.
My final straw broke,
left choking on my misery.
Alone I lay,
me and my gun.
All my life,
waiting for death to come.

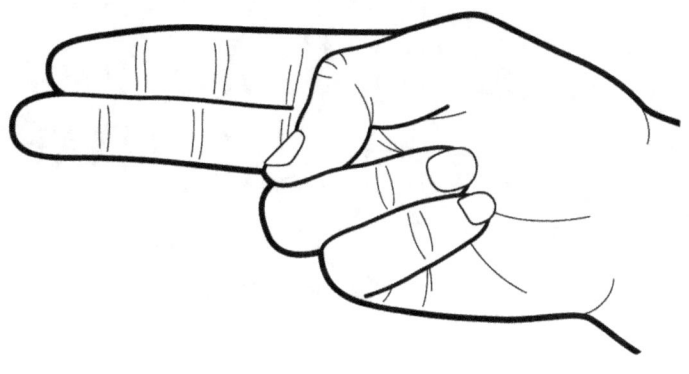

WINGS

I watch you from afar,
through my lens,
through my window.
An angel, your wings unfolded,
embracing the weakened form,
not worthy of your touch.
I wait for your mercy,
I yearn to be embraced,
begging for your celestial suffocation.

WITCH

Her face comes to me in my dreams,
a lucid pleasure, enticing.
The mistress from the forest,
from the heart of nature.
She smells of everglades,
and tortured souls.
Her touch is electric,
shocking my every nerve.
Her body flexes and mesmerises,
hypnotised from her beguiling eyes.
Her song keeps me dreaming,
silencing my internal cries.
I don't want to wake,
wrap me in your mortuary arms,
your voodoo charms,
my witch from the dream world.

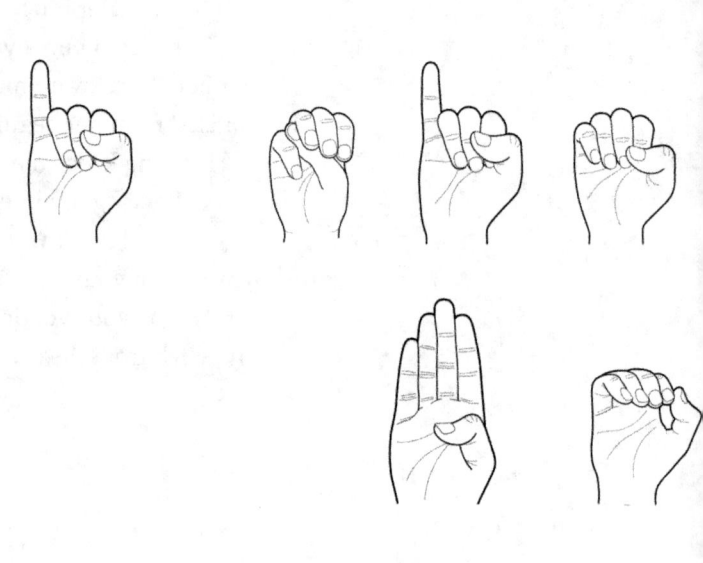

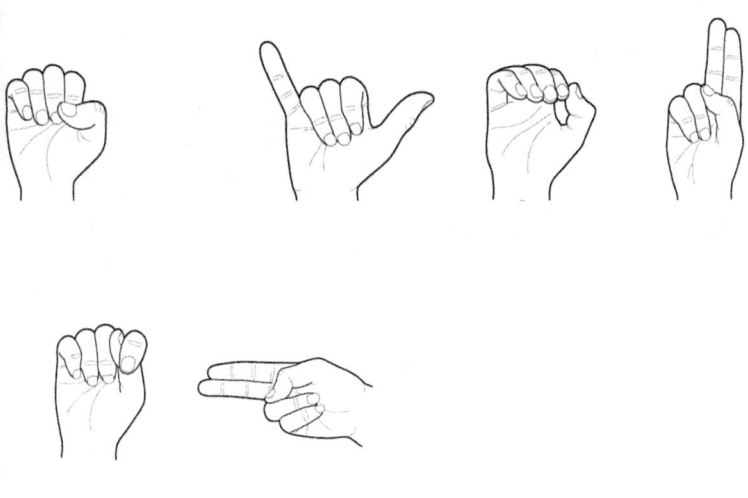

ABOUT THE AUTHOR

The author of Waiting for Death to Come, Leigh Haddington, can be found lurking around Leeds, England. Husband and a father of two, most of his time is taken up with his full-time job and growing veg (not this has anything to do with his writing).

Raised on a diet of video nasties in the very early eighties, a teenage life of metal and horror films, with the drippings of horror books from King and Herbert, Leigh developed a twisted world that wouldn't look lost on an Alice Cooper album.

        facebook.com/leighhaddington
        twitter.com/leighhaddington
        instagram.com/leigh.haddington

ALSO BY LEIGH HADDINGTON

KINGS OF HELL

"Better to reign in Hell than serve in Heaven."

Lucifer in *Paradise Lost* by John Milton

Desperate to save her son's life, Jude Fitzroy, signs a contract with the devil. She gets to raise Nick until he is eighteen and then Lucifer will take his place - she will never know the difference, and Nick will rule Hell in Lucifer's stead.

A life swap with the King of Hell wasn't how Nick saw his future but the past had sealed his fate. Now, not only does he have power and magic beyond his wildest dreams, but also a life that is dragging him through his worst nightmares.

In a world where Hell is on the doorstep of everyone's life, Nick discovers just how far he will have to go for his family, freedom and a future of being himself. Lucifer, however, has other ideas and will do anything to keep the contract in place.

EMOTION CORROSION

In between family life, work life and author life I get these poems forming in my head.

They wriggle, squirm and prod till I let them out. I squeeze them, manipulate them and push them through my fingers to the screen.

They drag themselves into words from the media into your open, willing mind. They dig deep, embed themselves into your world, your life, your dreams.

Enjoy my gifts to you...

Forever.

www.ingramcontent.com/pod-product-compliance
Lightning Source LLC
Chambersburg PA
CBHW071532080526
44588CB00011B/1654